While i thought
that i was learning
how to live,
i have been learning
how to die.

Leonardo Da Vinci

There will be no big introduction to this book, as you may be used to. I will not talk about purposes in life, discipline, health, and all that stuff. Just be kind to everybody. The rest is up to you. If you want to achieve financial freedom, just do it. We will start right off.

This book does not guarantee that this method will work, but I think it is an important lesson for many young people who do not know that they can get rich with simple steps. So, this is just a theory that I want to share, which makes sense and has lots of proof throughout the internet. You may already know all of the following steps. Good for you. But there are many who don't.

Quick introduction: I am a 25-year-old passionate filmmaker and entrepreneur living in Germany. While writing this, I am sitting on a train from Frankfurt to Berlin, a 5-hour trip. I am not rich at the moment, but that is just another case. Maybe I will publish more of my thoughts later in my life, but for now, this should be enough.

So, let's start.

STEP 1 - FIX CALCULATOR

How much money do you need to take care of your fixed costs?

Firstly, you need to understand fixed costs. They contain all the costs that you can't change but need to pay monthly to live. Then you have variable costs, costs which can be lowered based on how much value they have on you.

Fixed costs include rent, food, and drink.
Variable costs include travel and fun.

The key question is: What do you really NEED? For instance, do you need to eat out every day? (Personally, I dislike eating at restaurants because everything tastes better at home, and it also saves you money.)

Regarding fun, I understand if you want to go out with your friends. But if you have real and good friends, they will always support you if you tell them that you are in a „hustling" mode and don't want to go out more than one or two times a week. If you can handle less, good for you.

As for travel, if you have a car, do you really need it? I will come back to this later. For now, let's do a quick calculation.

Example 1:

Kevin is living with his parents. He doesn't need to take care of rent or food because everything is provided by his beloved parents.
Kevin needs €30 for his phone contract and €30 for the gym or sports.
On average, he spends €140 for car insurance,
€100 for fuel,
€350 for going out with friends,
and €150 for eating out.

This is just a quick example, and you can add your rent, children's costs, etc. to it. It's just to simplify the strategy.

So Kevin NEEDS €60 per month.
His variable costs are €740,
making his total €800.

But does he really need a car? What if he spends €60 on a monthly ticket?
That would save him €180 in variable costs.
He could also reduce going out with friends to half, or €170.
I would say that €150 for eating out is okay because of inflation nowadays.
Sometimes, parents are working and you have to eat outside.
And sometimes you just want to; that's okay.

So now the costs would be:

NEEDS: €60
Variables: €380
Total: €440 -> Let's round it up to €500.

With €500, Kevin could still be happy and live his average life.
If you are disciplined enough and you really WANT to hustle, you could even save more and quit more stuff. (If you need new trousers or a shirt, you will find stuff for €20-30 on the internet. Nobody cares about brands.)
But for now, let's work with this €500. From now on, this is going to be our deadline.

You need to organize €500 per month to be okay. What can you do? Work. Just go to work.

STEP 2 - SAVE FOR YOUR BUSINESS

At this point, we need 500€ a month to take care of ourselves.
We do NOT NEED any profession in a field to get this. It is okay if it takes a bit.
Don't stress yourself. You don't live to stress yourself.
I don't know where I read this and who said this, but this quote is very important:

„Slow is smooth and smooth is fast."

You will not achieve anything if you are doing things with haste.
Just lower your stress level and don't think about it. Just make things happen.

Find a job. Find a full-time job.
That means you are working 40 hours a week.
You get paid around 12€/hr at a very basic job.
You end up with about 1200€ in your bank account.
Now you have still 700€ left after fixed costs.

If you have someone you trust and love, give them the 700€ every month and tell them not to give it back to you until you need it to invest. After 10 months, you are left with 7K€.

A month has 720 hours. You spend 240 for sleeping (8h/day), 160 for your job, and about 160 for travel, eating, and having fun.
You have 160 hours left in a month,
awake.

As I told you, this is not a book to tell you to be productive or do this and that exercise.
If it is essential to you, you will use your time correctly from now on.
If not, YOU DON'T WANT TO BECOME RICH.

What do I do now with these 160 hours left?

I will tell you.

STEP 3 - FIND A PRODUCT

This is as simple as it is written here. Find a product to sell.
If you have any interests or knowledge in any field, this is better for you. But we need a product to sell.
Analyze your surroundings. What do your neighbors, family, or citizens use?
Let's take a wall clock as an example.
I am sorry that I don't have any better examples, but it's 1 am, I'm still sitting on the train, and this should work as an example.

A wall clock costs about 15-20€ on average. You might think, „Oh, that's cheap."
Yes, that is what we are searching for.
We need a product that sells quickly without overthinking or regretting spending „only" 15-20€ on a product that might look cool or have a cool function in it.

Why did I mention the 160 hours?

STEP 4 - RESEARCH

We will start using our time.
Get home after work. Chill. Be happy. Be motivated. Eat something.
Get to your phone, laptop, PC, or whatever device you have access to the internet with.

Find out the details about:

Who uses wall clocks?
What places buy wall clocks?
Where can you sell wall clocks?
How much competition do you have?
What can you do better than others?
Do you have somebody in your neighborhood, family, or any kind of relationship who might be interested in something like this?
The first summarized question is: Is there any market or can I create a need for this product?

Don't stress yourself. There is always a way. If you believe in your product and yourself, you will work it out. Use your time to research.

The second summarized question is: What product do I want to buy?

How does it have to look?
What special features does it need?
How do I name it?

Of course, you can imagine more questions. These are just examples to get you on the right track.

The third summarized question is: Where do I buy it?

What do I want to spend?
Do I have room for storage?
Where is a manufacturer for wall clocks?
Is there any manufacturer nearby so I can take a look at the process?
Compare sellers.

The fourth question is: Where do I sell it?

Are there any special marketplaces for my product?
Are there any friends or family members who want to buy my product?
Are there any blogs for my product?
Are there any stores that might be interested in selling it for me for a percentage?

Suggestion:

If you want to charge the customer 20€, the product should cost you
(including shipping costs from the manufacturer to your storage): 5-7€.
Try to use the 300% rule.
If a product costs you 1€, sell it for 4€.
So you are left with about 2€ after taxes.

STEP 5 - 10 MONTH LATER

Ten months later, you have saved €7,000. You have found a supplier and already established your marketplace/network to sell the product. Let's say the wall clock costs €5, so you can buy 1,400 wall clocks for €7,000. You have prepared everything and can now start selling.

IMPORTANT: As I told you, don't stress! It is okay if you don't sell out in the first month. Use your time to acquire customers.

DO NOT TOUCH THE MONEY OF YOUR REVENUE. STEP 1 IS KEY!

Remember: Now that you have spent the money that you saved up for the products, you can still save the money that is on top of your fixed costs and invest it in advertisements. You have a smartphone, take cool pictures. Watch some YouTube videos about how to create an ad campaign. It's easy if you really want to sell something.

STEP 6 - REPEAT

Imagine it took you 8 months to sell out. Now, how much money should you have made? Let's say you used half of your additional money on ads.

Costs:
€7,000 on products.
€2,100 on ads and selling strategies.

Revenue:
€28,000 from product sales.
€2,100 from leftovers after fixed costs from your job.

Total:
€30,100.

DO NOT JUST THINK ABOUT PROFIT.
This is the money that we've made and have right now in the bank for this product.
So now we repeat, but bigger.

You have easily made about €30k in 1.5 years. „Slow is smooth and smooth is fast."
Now that you have the knowledge of all the questions you needed to sell the product, you should
know exactly what kind of people you need to target for sales.

Now, take €30k for investment.
€30k at €5 for the product makes it: 6,000 units.
You should be able to sell out in at least half the time you needed at first.

Revenue now should be:
€120,000 from product sales.
€2,100 from leftovers after fixed costs from your job.

Total:
€122,100.

BOOM. You made €120k in under 2 years.

STEP 7 - QUIT YOUR JOB

Now, you need more time to scale it again. Take 12k from the revenue to take care of one year of your
fixed costs. Yes, you've leveled up your lifestyle. Now watch this.

STEP 8 - REPEAT

Take the 120K. Put 100K in product costs and 20K in ads and selling strategies. (You should know
your clients and costs better now, so it might all be variable.) Use your time and ask more questions. If
your client field is already saturated, try changing locations to find customers. Let's do the math.

Now that you are buying for 100K€, your supplier could lower the price to at least 0.50€ per piece:

100k invested at 4.50€ is 22,222 products.

Revenue:
444K€.

STEP 9 - REPEAT

The math goes on and on.
I think you should have understood the strategy that I wanted to tell you in this book.
With step 9, you should become a millionaire.
You're welcome.

STEP 10 - FIND SOMETHING NEW

Now that you've figured out a system that works best for you, repeat it.
Show it to friends. Be happy. Do things you love.
Be financially free.

ALWAYS BE AWARE OF STEP 1!
IF YOU LOSE SIGHT OF STEP 1, YOU WILL BE DANGERED
TO BE BROKE AGAIN.

There is a German saying: „Money is on the street, you just need to collect it."
I am still sitting in the train that I mentioned in the beginning.
It's 01:43 AM now. I started writing this at 00:02 AM.
Actually, I thought it would take 10 pages to write it all down, but it only took 7.
But it took me 10 years to learn this lesson.

Let's see where my journey takes me. The world is ours.
I'm dreaming of shooting my first films this year. Life is all about stories.
Maybe someday someone will read this in front of me, or maybe nobody will ever read this.
But I wrote it down because I just like doing things I think.

Sincerely yours,

Farhad Tahir

People love
chopping wood.
In this activity one
immediately sees
results.

Albert Einstein

I don't care that they stole
my idea...
I care that they don't have
any
of their own.

Nikola Tesla

PROGRESS

PROGRESS

PROGRESS

PROGRESS

PROGRESS

PROGRESS

PROGRESS

PROGRESS

PROGRESS

PROGRESS

PROGRESS

PROGRESS

PROGRESS

PROGRESS